WILD HORSES

Contents

The Struggle to Survive

They burst through the morning mist, galloping across the rough countryside. They are wild horses, born to a life of speed, beauty, and freedom.

These horses can be found all over the world. Some, such as the Przewalski's horse from Mongolia, have adapted over many thousands of years to suit their environments. In England, the wild Exmoor ponies are an ancient breed that made their home on the barren moors when England was still part of mainland Europe during the last ice age.

Others, such as the Kaimanawa wild horses in New Zealand and the brumbies in Australia, were brought from their original homes in Europe to strange foreign lands by early explorers and settlers.

Exmoor Pony

Brumbies

Kaimanawa
Wild Horses

3

In North and South America, the wild *mustangs* that race across the plains have a history of their own.

The small herd of wild mustangs crosses the *badlands* of southern Montana, searching for new grass. The horses are hungry and exhausted after a long, snowy winter.

Fences, north and south of the badlands, keep the horses from the better grasslands reserved for cattle grazing. The grey *stallion* inspects every kilometre of fence for an opening. He can smell the sweet grass, but it is just out of reach.

Suddenly, the lead *mare* catches the scent of a mountain lion. Her whinny of alarm quickly alerts the rest of the herd, and she leads a *stampede* across the rugged

badlands. The stallion follows them to hurry up any stragglers. By fording a flooding creek, they escape the hungry cat.

The young horses, though some are only a month old, will always remember the smell of the fearsome cat.

The horses regroup at a familiar spring several kilometres away. They know the location of every water source in the badlands.

While the horses graze on the sparse grass, the young *colts* and *fillies* run and play, returning often to their mothers to nurse.

These first few months of life are very important to the young *foals*. They will need to grow strong and healthy during the short summer if they are to avoid predators and live through the freezing winter ahead.

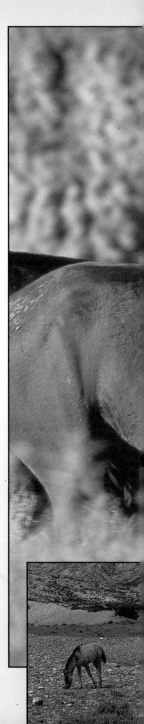

Like wild horses everywhere, the wild
horses of North America are survivors.
Their small, sturdy bodies are perfectly
suited to getting the most out of the sparse
food. Their strong hooves – which are
sometimes three times as thick as those
of other horses – carry them safely
over rocky outcrops, and their
speed and cunning help them avoid
nature's hunters.

They have adapted well for newcomers.
The wild horses that race across the
plains of North America, today, are
relatively recent immigrants to the
continent. To understand their sometimes
strange journey, we need to look far
back in time.

Horses of Long Ago

Horses first wandered through North America millions of years ago, and crossed back and forth over the *Bering Land Bridge*. These early horses were tough enough to live on the often sparse grass, and fast enough to outrun hungry sabre-toothed tigers and giant wolves.

More than a million years ago, a herd of these horses drowned trying to cross the flooded Snake River near the present-day town of Hagerman, Idaho. Today, people can imagine how these horses looked by studying their fossilized skeletons.

Horses had seemed to be permanent inhabitants in North and South America but, about 10,000 years ago, they mysteriously disappeared. Perhaps, they were wiped out by disease or *parasites*. Perhaps, early people hunted them to *extinction*. But something happened, and the horses were gone.

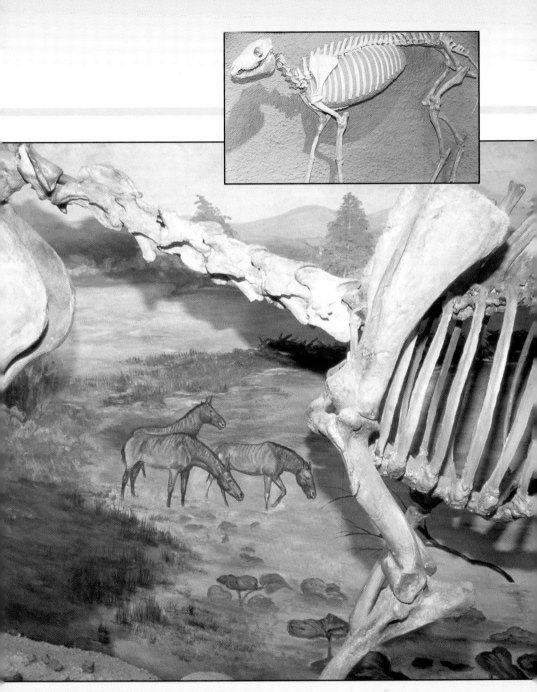

11

Horses didn't return to North America until 1519, when Spanish *conquistadores* started bringing them across the Atlantic to explore new Spanish colonies. At first, Native Americans feared the horses, which they called "sky dogs".

These horses, called Andalusians, were very different from the small, striped, stocky horses that had roamed the continent 10,000 years before. The Andalusians had the fine features, speed, and toughness of desert-bred Arabians, and the large size of European warhorses.

To the Europeans who settled in North America, the horses were more valuable than gold. But the wide open grasslands tempted the horses and, over the years, many escaped.

The herds of *mesteños*, or mustangs, as they are called today, quickly grew until millions of wild horses thundered across the West.

The tough little horses that made up these huge herds dramatically changed the lives of the Native Americans who lived across the Great Plains. By the 1600s, these tribes owned thousands of mustangs.

Of these tribes, the Comanche were known for their horsemanship, and the Cayuse and Nez Percé for their skills in breeding quality horses.

In fact, by the time explorers Meriwether Lewis and William Clark arrived in Nez Percé territory in 1805, the tribe had perfected a new breed of horse. The Nez Percé believed that horses were a gift from their gods, and that the most valuable horses were those with beautifully spotted coats. Today, these horses are known as Appaloosas.

A Western Round-up

Sunrise breaks over the Continental Divide. A *band* of wild horses stirs restlessly on the northern edge of the Great Divide Basin. The cool, dry morning is free of any coyote scent. But trouble is in the air.

The *bay* stallion, standing aloof on a rise, knows it. The mares know it.

Suddenly the air is filled with the roar of a large, black helicopter swooping out of the sky towards them. The horses stampede across Wyoming's high desert. Their thundering hooves churn up a choking cloud of dust.

The lead mare breaks towards the rough terrain of the badlands, the stallion following, pushing the lagging foals to run still faster. The helicopter hovers noisily just behind them.

Suddenly, horses and riders with flying ropes jump out from behind the stampeding herd. The terrified wild horses scatter.

A *roan* mare and her filly slip into a small canyon. The others follow the lead mare as she races away, and into the trap. Clang! A gate locks behind them as they crash against a hard fence.

Crazed, the entrapped horses jump and kick wildly. With a final surge of strength, the stallion leaps skyward, hurling himself over the steel gate. He looks back at his herd, but the pull of freedom is too strong.

Exhausted, he trots away and rejoins the mare and foal that escaped earlier. The morning sun warms their sweaty backs as they move off again into the badlands.

The world of the wild horse has changed dramatically over the past 100 years. Following the Indian Wars of the late 1800s, the mustangs were slaughtered by the thousands and were later used for pet food. By the mid-1900s, they were almost extinct.

Today, wild horses in the United States are protected by The Free-Roaming Wild Horse and Burro Act of 1971, and their numbers are up to about 40,000.

But because the vast, open prairies where they roam have shrunk so dramatically, their populations have to be managed by round-ups. The youngest horses are selected for sale, and go to buyers for *domestication*.

Island Horses

The wild horses of the western United States are not the only ones feeling the crush of civilization. Just off the coasts of Virginia and Maryland, small bands of horses have carved out a life on narrow, sandy islands that rise just a few feet above the Atlantic Ocean.

Legend has it that some of these horses are descended from horses that escaped Spanish shipwrecks over 300 years ago. Others were abandoned by British ships pirating gold from the Spanish. And others were brought over by early colonists.

Whatever their origin, the wild horses of these barrier islands are some of the hardiest in the world. Once, when some mustangs were introduced to increase the size of the herd, most of the mustangs died – just as many of the first horses to arrive probably did.

The horses that were tough enough to survive passed on their traits to their offspring. Their bodies are stunted by the lack of nourishing food. Their coats are shaggy, protecting them from freezing storms in the winter and from blood-hungry insects in the summer.

In fact, these small, wild island horses survive so well that they constantly run the danger of overpopulating their small home. That is why, during every July since 1920, the Chincoteague Volunteer Fire Company rounds up all of the *ponies* and auctions off some of the foals.

Unfortunately, the journey to the sale ring includes a forced swim across an ocean channel, and can be hazardous for foals that are too young to make the swim.

Science and Wild Horses

It is sunrise. Dr Kirkpatrick spots the band of sorrel and *pinto* mares grazing on frost-covered grasses, and identifies which mares need to be treated.

Moving slowly to avoid spooking the horses, he loads his single-shot dart gun with a dose of *vaccine* and begins to move in. He then approaches a beautiful sorrel mare that has just foaled.

Taking careful aim, he squeezes the trigger. Crack! A bright orange dart hits her hindquarters, injecting the vaccine. The dart self-ejects and falls to the ground.

To the mare, it doesn't feel like much more than an insect bite. She runs a few metres and then stops to look back, trying to work out what just happened.

With 55 more mares to treat, Dr Kirkpatrick heads over the frozen sand dunes of the barrier island, looking for his next patient. Dr Kirkpatrick is working with the National Park Service to find an alternative to the stressful and sometimes dangerous round-up method of controlling wild-horse populations.

The National Park Service has a plan in place to manage the population of 170 wild horses living on Assateague Island. Over the next few days, Dr Kirkpatrick will try to vaccinate all 56 mares to prevent them becoming pregnant before the next breeding season. The treatments can be given in the horses' own environment, with no need to round them up or capture them.

At last, after hours of work, Dr Kirkpatrick has vaccinated the final mare of the day. He smiles as he watches the horses gallop away, content, beautiful, and wild.

Glossary

badlands – an area that has sparse vegetation, and rocky land sculptured by erosion

band – a small group of animals

bay – a horse with a reddish brown coat and black legs, mane, and tail

Bering Land Bridge – a land bridge that connected Asia and North America during the last ice age

colt – a male horse less than four years old

conquistadores – Spanish explorers from the sixteenth century who conquered lands in America, Mexico, and Peru

domestication – the act of training or taming an animal

extinction – describes a species of animal that has died out

filly – a female horse less than four years old

foal – a male or female horse less than one year old

mare – a female horse that is old enough to breed

mesteño – the Spanish word for "stray"; thought to be where "mustang" comes from

mustang – a small, tough, wild horse found in western North America and South America

parasite – an organism that lives off, and often weakens or sickens, another organism

pinto – describes a horse with hair in large patches of white and another colour

pony – a size classification for a horse that measures no more than 14.2 hands (147.32 cm) at the top of the shoulder

roan – describes a horse that has a dark coat that is thickly mixed with white hair

sorrel – describes a horse with a reddish brown coat and similar or lighter colour mane and tail

stallion – a male horse that is old enough to breed

stampede – a panicked rush of frightened animals

vaccine – a medicine that helps prevent disease, or prevents pregnancy

About Buck Wilde

My childhood dream of living with wild horses recently came true when I set out through the West's most scenic badlands to photograph these beautiful animals. I'd like to thank Roy Packer of the Bureau of Land Management, who made finding the wild horses much easier than I'd imagined. Roy has worked since 1977 to preserve the wild-horse habitat in Wyoming, and he took me to some of their grazing and watering places.

There were many mustangs in the Great Divide Basin. A grey stallion, which became my favourite, was the first to spot me. Eventually, he signalled the mares and foals to leave the safety of the junipers, and I could see the whole band. That's when I really began to learn about wild horses around the world.

I'd also like to thank Rebecca Weber, whose love of wild horses helped shape this book.

Wild Horses

ISBN 13: 978-1-57-257670-4
ISBN 10: 1-57-257670-7

Mc Graw Hill **Kingscourt**

Published by:
McGraw-Hill Education
Shoppenhangers Road, Maidenhead, Berkshire, England, SL6 2QL
Telephone: 44 (0) 1628 502730
Fax: 44 (0) 1628 635895
Website: www.kingscourt.co.uk
Website: www.mcgraw-hill.co.uk

Written By **Buck Wilde**
Photographed by **Buck Wilde**
Edited by **Rebecca Weber**
Designed by **Mary C. Walker**

Additional photography by The Appaloosa Horse Club: (black and white Appaloosa, front cover, title page, p.7, p.17, p.25, p.30; Chief Joseph and Nez Percé tribe, p.15); Charlene Bechen (two Appaloosas touching noses, p.14); The Dominion Newspaper of Wellington, New Zealand: (Kaimanawa wild horses, pp. 2-3); Photobank: (Exmoor Pony, p.2; Brumbies, p.3)

Original Edition © 1997Shortland Publications Inc.
English Reprint Edition © 2010 McGraw Hill Publishing Company